M000017960

This Notebook

Belongs To:

____

Made in United States
Orlando, FL
07 August 2022

20672074R00083